THE LIVING FESTIVALS SERIES

Jack Priestley — Series Editor

Passover

LYNNE SCHOLEFIELD

RMEP

RELIGIOUS AND MORAL EDUCATION PRESS

Religious and Moral Education Press
An Imprint of Arnold-Wheaton
Hennock Road, Exeter EX2 8RP

A Division of E. J. Arnold & Son Ltd
Parkside Lane, Leeds LS11 5TD

A subsidiary of Pergamon Press Ltd
Headington Hill Hall, Oxford OX3 0BW

Pergamon Press Inc.
Maxwell House, Fairview Park, Elmsford, New York 10523

Pergamon Press Canada Ltd
Suite 104, 150 Consumers Road, Willowdale, Ontario M2J 1P9

Pergamon Press (Australia) Pty Ltd
P.O. Box 544, Potts Point, N.S.W. 2011

Pergamon Press GmbH
Hammerweg 6, D-6242 Kronberg, Federal Republic of Germany

First published 1982, reprinted 1983, 1985

Printed in Great Britain by A. Wheaton & Co. Ltd, Exeter

ISBN 0 08-027867-1 non net
        0 08-027868-X net

Dedicated to all my Jewish friends, with thanks.

ACKNOWLEDGEMENTS

The author and publisher wish to thank the following organizations who kindly provided photographs: Camera Press Ltd; Jewish Programme Materials Project; Keystone Press Ltd; University of London, The Warburg Institute.

The words and music for the Passover songs appear by kind permission of Penguin Books Ltd in whose book *A Passover Haggadah* they originally appeared.

The author and series editor together accept full responsibility for all statements made in this book. They would, however, like to place on record their appreciation to Mr Clive Lawton B.A., of the Board of Deputies of British Jews, for reading the book in manuscript form and making helpful suggestions.

Cover photograph by courtesy of the Council of Christians and Jews.

Contents

Introduction

Imagine a smell or the taste of certain foods which bring back memories. It might be fresh-baked bread or newly-ground coffee or a turkey roasting in the oven.

Every year in a Jewish home the sight, smell and taste of certain foods bring back memories of a story. It is a story of freedom and Jews relive it every spring. Spring is the time of year for thinking about new life and for being joyful about it.

Passover (or Pesach as it is more accurately called) is all about new life — new life for a whole people, the Jews; new life for a country, Israel; and a new way of life for individual Jews all over the world. This new way of life is based on the Jewish law, the Torah.

1

The Celebrations

In every country where Jews live there are slightly different customs at festival times. This book is about the way Passover might be celebrated in a Jewish home in Britain. The Jewish calendar is different from the calendar most people in Britain follow but Passover usually takes place around April, in the Jewish month of Nisan.

Preparations begin with the house being cleaned and any leaven removed. (Leaven is any substance which will make dough rise, such as yeast or self-raising flour.) Passover is also called the Feast of Unleavened Bread and during the eight days that it lasts no leaven ('chametz' is the Hebrew word) is allowed in the house.

To make sure that the house is free of chametz a search takes place on the evening before the festival begins. This is done with great care and ceremony. A candle is used for a light. Any piece of chametz which is found is swept up, usually with a feather, and is burnt the following morning. Sometimes one of the children will hide some small pieces of chametz and the search becomes the first of the Passover games involving all the family.

Before the game starts a blessing is said, usually by the father. This is a kind of prayer. It is quite short and is spoken in Hebrew. One of the blessings used most often in Judaism is:

Baruch ata Adōnoy, Elōhaynu melech ha-ōlom,
bōray pree ha-gafen.

Blessed are you, Lord our God, King of the
Universe who brings forth fruit from the vine.

Nearly every activity during Passover begins with a blessing. This is because the festival is a religious celebration. But it takes place at home, not in the synagogue, the Jewish place of worship. Nevertheless it follows carefully all the details in the Torah.

Judaism is all about following the Torah, the first five books of what Christians call the Old Testament; they are Genesis, Exodus, Leviticus, Numbers and Deuteronomy. The Book of Exodus tells the story of Moses and how he led the Israelites out of slavery and towards the Promised Land. It also contains many of the laws of God, including the Ten Commandments.

All the laws of the Torah show how God wants his people to live. They tell them how they should treat one another and, above all, how they should love God.

Every Jewish child knows the Shema. The words tell us what it means to be a Jew. They are recited every day in Hebrew. In English it reads:

Hear, O Israel, the Lord our God, the Lord is One, and you
shall love the Lord your God with all your heart and with all
your soul and with all your might.

Passover celebrates the way in which God freed the Jews from slavery in Egypt, led them to their own land and gave them the law through Moses so that the people would know how to love and worship him. Every year when children ask why they are looking for leaven or eating special foods, parents have a chance to retell the story. This has been happening for over three thousand years.

There are synagogue services to celebrate Passover but the Seder meal on the first or second evening of the festival takes place at home. It always follows a set order. This order is written down in a book called the Haggadah. 'Haggadah' means simply 'telling' or 'story'. The book contains all the words for the proper ordering of the meal which is a religious service. The Haggadah itself is always on the table with the other items.

Throughout the Seder meal many different things are going on. No one gets bored or forgotten. There are prayers, special things to eat from the Seder plate, questions for the youngest child to ask, a huge meal to be eaten, wine to drink, stories and singing.

Father reads from the Haggadah

9

The candles on the table are lit. The wine is poured out and a glassful is drunk for the first time while the blessing is said (wine is drunk at four different times during the Seder). Then Father breaks the matzo (the special unleavened bread) and passes a piece to everyone. Then each person reaches out and takes a small selection of green vegetables, usually parsley or lettuce, dips it in salt water and eats it.

At this point in the meal the 'four questions' are asked. The

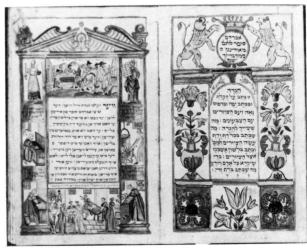

Ancient Haggadah

youngest child present stands up and asks why everything is different on Passover night. He asks:

1 'Why do we have unleavened bread?'
2 'Why do we eat bitter herbs?'
3 Why do we dip our herbs in salt water?'
4 'Why do we sit in a reclining position on cushions?'

Usually these questions are asked in Hebrew. Sometimes they are sung, either by the child on his own or with help from the other members of the family.

MA NISHTANA

Ma nish-ta-na ha-lai-lah ha-zeh mi-kol ha-lei - lot, mi-
- kol ha-lei - lot? She-b' - hol ha-lei-lot a - nu oh-lin 1.ha-
2.sh'-

- meitz _ u - ma - tzah, ha - meitz _ u - ma - tzah. Ha-
- ar_____ y' - ra - kot, sh' - ar_____ y' - ra kot. Ha-

- lai - lah ha-zeh, ha - lai- lah ha-zeh ku- lo _ ma - tzah, _ ha-
- lai - lah ha-zeh, ha - lai- lah ha-zeh ku- lo _ ma - ror, ____ ha-

- lai - lah ha-zeh ha - lai - lah ha-zeh ku- lo _ ma - tzah. 2.She-b'-
- lai - lah ha-zeh ha - lai- lah ha-zeh ku- lo _ ma - ror.

3. She-b'-hol ha-lei-lot ein a-nu mat-bi-lin a-fi-lu pa-am e-hat.
   Ha-lai-lah ha-zeh, ha-lai-lah ha-zeh sh'-tei f'a-a-mim.

4. She-b'-hol ha-lei-lot a-nu oh-lin bein yosh-vin u-vein m'-su-bin.
   Ha-lai-lah ha-zeh, ha-lai-lah ha-zeh ku-la-nu m'-su-bin.

It is the father of the family who has to reply. He begins to tell the story of how God brought the Israelites out of slavery in Egypt into the freedom of the Promised Land.

While he speaks he points to the foods on the Seder dish. At the appropriate places in the story the bitter herbs are eaten, with a piece of matzo and sometimes with the sweet, sticky charoset.

After the main meal has been eaten, more prayers are said and the third and fourth glasses of wine are drunk. The Seder ends with singing. This usually consists of folk-songs which tell the Passover story in another way.

The story, which has been handed down for thousands of years and which Passover still celebrates, is told in detail in the next chapter.

DAYEINU

I - lu ho-tzi ho-tzi - a - nu, ho-tzi-a - nu mi-mitz-ra-yim,

ho - tzi - a - nu mi-mitz - ra - yim da - yei - nu.

Chorus

Da - da - yei - nu, ____ da - da - yei - nu, ____ da - da - yei - nu, da -

1, 2   3

- yei - nu da-yei - nu da - yei - nu. yei - nu da-yei - nu.

2. I-lu na-tan, na-tan la-nu, na-tan la-nu et ha-sha-bat, na-tan la-nu et ha-sha-bat, dayeinu. (Chorus).

3. I-lu na-tan, na-tan la-nu, na-tan la-nu et ha-to-rah, na-tan la-nu et ha-to-rah, dayeinu. (Chorus).

12

2

The Story

This is the way in which the telling of the Passover story begins:

> Youngest child: *'Why is this night different from all other nights?'*
> Father: (uncovers matzos) *'We were slaves to Pharaoh in Egypt and the Lord our God brought us out from there with a strong hand and an outstretched arm. . .'*

The story is set out in the Haggadah (the 'telling') and is usually told by the eldest male Jew present at the Seder. It includes the details which are in the Book of Exodus along with the comments and teachings of various rabbis. These are the teachers who through the centuries have tried to deepen the Jewish understanding of history and the way it is related to the present.

> Father: *'If God had not brought out our forefathers, then Jews today and in the future might still have been slaves. The story of our departure is well worth telling and so each year our children ask about it and learn the way God freed us from Egypt.*
> *'The Torah speaks about four sons who ask the questions in different ways. The first son is wise and asks about the*

13

meaning of laws which God has given us. *We can explain all the details of Pesach to him. The wicked son says, "What is the meaning of the service to* you?" *He excludes himself from the Seder and so really he excludes himself from the freedom too. The simple son asks, "What is this?" and you can give him a simple answer: "With a strong hand God brought us out of Egypt, from slavery". For the son who can't even ask a question you must still tell him that Pesach celebrates how God freed us from Egypt.'*

Us not *them.* Try to imagine that you are reliving that night when the Jews left Egypt.

'We hadn't always been there. God chose Abraham and made a covenant with him. He had to leave his home and the idol worship behind, and God made him the father of a new nation. He had a son, Isaac, and two grandsons, Jacob and Esau. One of Jacob's sons was Joseph and it was he who brought the whole family to Egypt. God had told Abraham that there would be a time of slavery and oppression but that they would come through it. They would be saved. He was right, but it didn't happen only once. There have been many times of oppression and the need for salvation (here the speaker raises his cup of wine).

'In Egypt the Jews grew in numbers and perhaps that frightened the Egyptians; they thought we might fight against them. They made us slaves and forced us to do their labouring and building. But that wasn't enough for the Pharaoh. He ordered that every new-born baby boy was to be thrown into the River Nile. When Moses was born his parents hid him and then made a floating crib so he wouldn't drown in the river. He was found by the Pharaoh's daughter and was brought up by her as an Egyptian prince.

'Years later Moses saw what was happening to his own people and he killed a cruel Egyptian. He was forced to leave, but returned to Egypt after many years for God had promised

14

Ancient Egypt

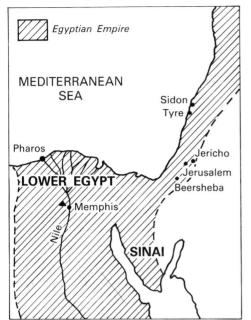

Present-day Israel

15

that he would bring his people out with a strong arm and with signs and wonders. There were the plagues, the Angel of Death, the journey through the desert, and the law given to Moses on Mount Sinai.

'Moses confronted Pharaoh, asking him to release the Jewish slaves but the king wouldn't give up his workforce. Then strange things started to happen. First there was the plague of blood, then frogs. They only affected the Egyptians. God had made a division, so in Goshan, where Jews lived, there were no frogs or anything else. Each time, Pharaoh gave way and said we could go, and then when the plague stopped he said we couldn't. In the end there was a final, terrible plague. The first-born of every Egyptian household was to die.

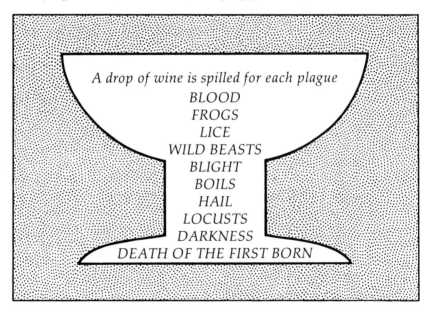

A drop of wine is spilled for each plague
BLOOD
FROGS
LICE
WILD BEASTS
BLIGHT
BOILS
HAIL
LOCUSTS
DARKNESS
DEATH OF THE FIRST BORN

'Moses gave instructions for us to kill a lamb and put some of the blood around the door. "When the Angel of Death comes," said Moses, "he will see the blood and pass over the house." And so it was. In every Egyptian house someone died. The Egyptians were terrified and urged Moses to take the Jews away as fast as possible.

'Following Moses' instructions everyone had packed their things and had eaten a special meal the night before — some of the lamb, unleavened bread and bitter herbs. Early in the morning with that day's bread still unrisen we left.'

THE EXODUS

Therefore let us rejoice
At the wonder of our deliverance,
From bondage to freedom,
From agony to joy,
From mourning to festivity,
From darkness to light,
From slavery to redemption
Before God let us sing a new song.

(words from the Haggadah)

That is the end of the Passover story but it is not the end of the story of freedom. Moses led the Jews safely across the Red Sea (the Egyptian pursuers were drowned) and into the desert. There were many more problems and many more miracles before the Promised Land was reached. That itself is the beginning of another story which is still continuing. In the desert, at Sinai, Moses received the Torah and a new covenant was made between God and his chosen people, an agreement that is renewed every year at Passover.

The Seder meal ends with these words:

'The redemption is not yet complete. . .
Peace, shalom. . .
Next year in Jerusalem,
Next year may all be free.'

3

The Passover Symbols

Many of the objects and activities which occur in the Seder seem to be there so that someone will ask, 'Why?' The order of the meal gives every opportunity for probing further and further into the meanings behind what is being done.

Some of the answers to the questions are written in the Haggadah. When the youngest child asks the 'four questions' the story is told in great detail. The meaning of each of the special foods is explained. The reason for drinking wine on four different occasions is given.

But as well as all these traditional answers each individual family will have other, more personal meanings to give. There may be in the family more recent examples of freedom. Some of these may be about the dreadful time before and during the Second World War when many Jewish families suffered persecution in Europe. A few survived or escaped and found new freedom in Israel and other countries. The word 'Exodus' was often used again at that time. Today many Jews are trying to escape to freedom from other parts of the world. So at Passover time, especially, Jews think and talk about these things and the hope for peace in the future.

For all this the basic symbols remain the same. Passover is also the Feast of Unleavened Bread. It lasts for seven or eight days and during this time no leavened bread is eaten, only

Jewish immigrants arrested while illegally attempting to enter Israel in 1947

matzo. During the Seder the question is always asked, 'Why do we eat matzos?' The answer is always the same:

'We eat matzos because we had to leave Egypt in a hurry. There wasn't time to bake bread with yeast in. We ate the unleavened bread with the roasted lamb and the bitter herbs. We were packed and dressed for the journey, ready to go at midnight.'

Notice how always Jews refer to their ancestors as 'we'. *'We* eat matzos.' *'We* had to leave Egypt in a hurry.' It is this real sense of belonging which is at the heart of everything which Jews believe and do. Passover is, in every way, a family celebration. A Jew feels related to every other Jew in the world and to every other Jew in history.

Jews in the Soviet Union face many restrictions. Here Jewish women are buying matzos despite the possibility of arrest

In giving his answer to the 'four questions' the Jewish father refers to the items on the Seder plate.

Lamb bone   Usually the shank bone of a lamb is used. This is a reminder of the lamb which was killed so that its blood could be painted on the doorposts and lintels of the slaves' huts in Egypt. It was the sign that the Angel of Death should *'pass over'*. It has also become a symbol of the strong arm of God taking care of his people, the Jews.

Egg   The egg is usually hard boiled and then 'roasted' in a flame for a few seconds. It is a symbol of new life. In some countries a hard-boiled egg forms the first course of the Passover meal.

Jewish families in some Eastern European countries keep up a tradition of painting the shells of these eggs with different patterns and colours. Sometimes one of the eggs is left

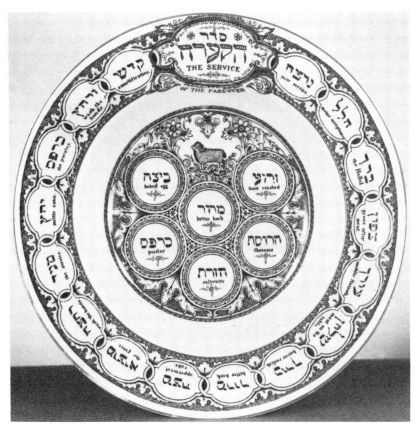

Seder dish

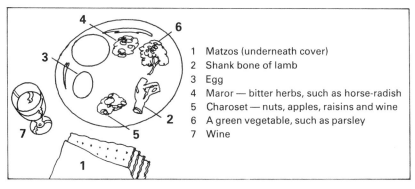

1 Matzos (underneath cover)
2 Shank bone of lamb
3 Egg
4 Maror — bitter herbs, such as horse-radish
5 Charoset — nuts, apples, raisins and wine
6 A green vegetable, such as parsley
7 Wine

Passover foods on the Seder dish

21

unboiled. Any child in the family who knows how that one is painted can have great fun playing tricks on other members of the family!

Green vegetable (karpas)   This is usually parsley or lettuce. It is a symbol of life and the way in which God provided for the Israelites in the wilderness, giving them food and water. At springtime it is also a reminder of the green fields — of the fact that growth has begun again and life goes on.

Bitter herbs (maror)   This is usually horse-radish, which has a bitter taste. It is intended to be a symbol of slavery. If it brings tears to your eyes so much the better. That will remind you that being a slave is always a terrible and bitter thing.

Charoset   This is a mixture of fruit, nuts, spices and wine. In contrast with the bitter herbs this mixture tastes sweet and pleasant. It is a symbol of the taste of freedom, which is always sweet. Some Jews also suggest that the brown, sticky mixture is a reminder of the mortar with which the slaves in Egypt had to make bricks.

CHAROSET

---

4 tablespoons chopped nuts
(walnuts, hazelnuts or almonds)
1 small cooking apple, grated
1 teaspoon cinnamon
a little wine

Mix all the ingredients together and bind into a paste with the wine. Form into a flat round shape and serve on the Seder Dish.

Salt water   Also on the Seder table is a bowl of salt water. The karpas is dipped into this during the Seder, as are the eggs if they are eaten as part of the meal. This represents the tears of pain and sorrow shed by the slaves before they were freed.

Wine During the meal wine is drunk at four different times. This is a reminder of the fourfold promise which God gave to Moses. It can be found in the Book of Exodus 6: 6–8. God promised that he would: (1) deliver them from slavery; (2) redeem them; (3) take them as his chosen people; (4) give them a land of their own.

4

Details of the Seder

Passover is not just a reminder of a story. In the past it was closely linked with agriculture and the spring, and it is also called the Feast of Unleavened Bread. The search for chametz is the climax of preparations to remove all leaven from the house. This begins with spring-cleaning when all leavened items are collected together and 'sold' to a non-Jew who keeps them during the festival. Afterwards they can be bought back. In many Jewish homes the ordinary crockery, cutlery, and cooking equipment are packed away and a special Passover set is used for the eight days.

These rules about food are called 'making things kosher'. This means 'fit' or 'right'. Many packaged goods carry the words 'kosher for Passover'. The basis for the rules can be found in the Torah. Exodus 13: 6–7 gives the Passover details.

This passage goes on to tell fathers that they must pass on the story to their sons. The Seder is the annual opportunity to do so. Everyone comes together at home in the family setting, often three generations together, to explain and learn what it is all about. Friends may be there too, especially if they are poor and cannot afford their own Seder. The order is flexible to take account of different needs, but during the meal there are several details which appeal especially to children.

When the middle matzo is broken at the beginning of the Seder one part is put aside and covered. It is the 'afikomen' — a Greek word meaning 'afterwards'. It is eaten at the end of the

A Jewish family at the Seder

meal and the Seder cannot be completed until it is eaten. The leader often hides the afikomen and the children have to find it. It is so important that the one who does discover it may claim a reward, either money or a present. It is then returned and is the last food tasted.

Also intriguing is the presence of Elijah's cup on the table. Elijah was a prophet in the Old Testament and there is a legend that he returns to earth dressed as a beggar to see whether people will receive him. Towards the end of the Seder a child is sent to open the door so that Elijah will know he is welcome. A cup of wine is waiting for him too. The Jews hope that one day God will complete the work of freedom begun in

Egypt by sending a specially chosen Messiah. Other prophets in the Old Testament said that Elijah would come first to prepare the people. There is a tradition that if every Jew faithfully kept just one Sabbath the Messiah would come. The leader of the Seder says:

> *'Elijah opens up for us the realm of mystery and wonder;*
> *Let us now open the door for Elijah.'*

After the meal the family does not leave the table. Instead they sing songs together mainly about Passover. Many of these folk-songs have words and phrases repeated again and again so even very young children can learn them. Probably the best known is called *Only one kid*.

HAD GADYA

One little goat, one little goat,
  My father bought for two zuzim.
One little goat, one little goat.
Then came a cat and ate the goat
  My father bought for two zuzim.
One little goat, one little goat.
Then came a dog and bit the cat,
  That ate the goat
My father bought for two zuzim.
  One little goat, one little goat.
Then came a stick and beat the dog,
  That bit the cat that ate the goat
My father bought for two zuzim.
  One little goat, one little goat.

Then came a fire and burned the stick,
  That beat the dog that bit the cat
That ate the goat
  My father bought for two zuzim.
One little goat, one little goat.

Then came the water and quenched the fire,
  That burned the stick that beat the dog
That bit the cat that ate the goat
  My father bought for two zuzim.
One little goat, one little goat.

Then came an ox and drank the water,
  That quenched the fire that burned the stick
That beat the dog that bit the cat
  That ate the goat
My father bought for two zuzim.
  One little goat, one little goat.

Then came a *shohet* and slaughtered the ox,
  That drank the water that quenched the fire
That burned the stick that beat the dog
  That bit the cat that ate the goat
My father bought for two zuzim.
  One little goat, one little goat.

Then came the angel of death and killed the *shohet,*
  That slaughtered the ox that drank the water
That quenched the fire that burned the stick
  That beat the dog that bit the cat
That ate the goat
  My father bought for two zuzim.
One little goat, one little goat.

Then came the Holy One, blessed be He,
  And slew the angel of death,
That killed the *shohet* that slaughtered the ox
  That drank the water that quenched the fire
That burned the stick that beat the dog
  That bit the cat that ate the goat
My father bought for two zuzim.
  One little goat, one little goat.

The singing can be enjoyed by everyone but at other times the words and ideas are more for the adults present. Each year something new may be understood about the salvation story. When the leader breaks the middle matzo he says:

'This is the bread of affliction'

Affliction means suffering, being in trouble, and Jewish families were not only 'in affliction' in Egypt. The story of Judaism is often one of oppression and persecution. Six million Jews died in Europe during the Second World War when Nazi leaders tried to kill every single Jew through the use of concentration and extermination camps. In many Jewish families there are no grandparents or uncles and aunts alive. In the 1930s and 1940s, when Passover was celebrated, Jews were tasting the bread of affliction in a very real way. When they said 'Now we are all still slaves. Next year may all be free', they knew that freedom would be very sweet indeed.

The Holocaust Museum, Jerusalem

28

This is the bread of affliction,
the poor bread,
which our fathers ate in the land
of Egypt.
Let all who are hungry come and eat.
Let all who are in want
share the hope of Passover.
As we celebrate here
we join with people everywhere.
This year we celebrate here.
Next year in the land of Israel.
Now we are still slaves.
Next year may all be free.

Freedom for the Jews has always been associated with Israel, the Promised Land, and each Passover ends with the words:

Next year in Jerusalem!
Next year may all be free!

The Western Wall, Jerusalem

In A.D. 70 the Jews were finally beaten by the Romans. Jerusalem, the symbol of Israel, was destroyed. For nearly nineteen hundred years there was a belief that one day the Jews would return to Israel. 'Next year in Jerusalem,' they said, and, indeed, following the Second World War, Israel once again became the Jewish homeland. The State of Israel was officially recognized in 1948.

Passover, then, can never simply be a happy occasion. There is too much of the dark side to the story. One rabbi taught that when the Egyptian armies were drowning in the sea the heavenly hosts broke out in songs of jubilation. God silenced them and said, 'My creatures are perishing, and you sing praises?' When the plagues are mentioned a drop of wine is spilled for each one — the cup of joy is lessened by the suffering of the Egyptians and they are remembered.

This is all in the past. What does Passover look forward to? The final words of the Seder sum this up:

Peace, Shalom
Peace for us! For everyone!
For all people, this, our hope:
Next year in Jerusalem!
Next year may all be free!

THINGS TO DO

1 Copy out the Shema and learn to recite it (see page 8).
2 Learn one of the songs associated with Passover and sing it.
3 Choose a title such as 'Freedom', 'Past and Present', or 'Celebration' and make a collage, or a drawing, or write a poem or story. You could make use of the Passover story or you could use other incidents from Jewish history.
4 Look up the Ten Commandments in Exodus 20: 1–17. These are part of the Torah. Discuss what they mean and the sort of attitudes and behaviour which they encourage.
5 Make a strip cartoon of the Passover story. You could do this individually or as a group doing one picture each and mounting them in order.
6 Make a display about Israel today, its history, places and people.
7 Try to answer these question as fully as you can:
   (a) Where does the name 'Passover' come from?
   (b) Which country is specially associated with the Jews?
   (c) What are the symbols used in the Seder to represent
           (i) new life
          (ii) bitterness of slavery
         (iii) sweet taste of freedom
   (d) Why is unleavened bread (matzo) eaten during Passover?
   (e) What is a blessing? Why are so many used in Jewish life?
   (f) Why do you think Jewish families go on remembering something which happened so long ago?

MATERIAL FOR TEACHERS

Useful addresses

Jewish Education Bureau
8 Westcombe Avenue
Leeds LS8 2BS

Council of Christians and Jews
48 Onslow Gardens
London SW7 3PX

The Jewish Museum
Woburn House
Upper Woburn Place
London WC1H 0EP

Books to read
Baskin, Leonard. *A Passover Haggadah*. Penguin, 1974.
Kossof, David. *Bible Stories*. Fontana, 1971.
Siegel and Strassfeld. *The First Jewish Catalogue*. Jewish
   Publication Society of America. (Obtainable from Rabbi D.
   Charing, Jewish Education Bureau.)

Workcards
Rankin, John. *Looking at Festivals*. Lutterworth.

Assembly books on festivals
Green, Victor. *Festivals and Saints Days*. Blandford.
Purton, Rowland. *Festivals and Celebrations*. Blackwell, 1979.
Smith, Harry. *Assemblies*. Heinemann, 1981.